YOUR KNOWLEDGE HAS VALUE

AF151330

Bibliographic information published by the German National Library:

The German National Library lists this publication in the National Bibliography; detailed bibliographic data are available on the Internet at http://dnb.dnb.de .

Imprint:

Copyright © 2015 GRIN Verlag, Open Publishing GmbH
Print and binding: Books on Demand GmbH, Norderstedt Germany
ISBN: 978-3-668-02096-2

This book at GRIN:

http://www.grin.com/en/e-book/303792/the-ethical-dilemma-of-valve-replacement-in-intravenous-drug-users

Antje Michel

The Ethical Dilemma of Valve Replacement in Intravenous Drug Users

Should Intravenous Drug Users be Offered a Second Valve Replacement?

GRIN Publishing

GRIN - Your knowledge has value

Since its foundation in 1998, GRIN has specialized in publishing academic texts by students, college teachers and other academics as e-book and printed book. The website www.grin.com is an ideal platform for presenting term papers, final papers, scientific essays, dissertations and specialist books.

Visit us on the internet:

http://www.grin.com/

http://www.facebook.com/grincom

http://www.twitter.com/grin_com

The Ethical Dilemma of Valve Replacement in Intravenous Drug Users:

Should

Intravenous Drug Users be Offered a Second Valve Replacement

Antje Michel

University of South Florida

Infective endocarditis (IE), brought on by introduction of pathogens into the bloodstream, is a serious, potentially lethal condition affecting approximately 12.7 out of 100,000 individuals annually (Bor et al., 2013). Complications of IE include stroke, organ damage, secondary infections, heart failure, and almost certain death if infected valves are not replaced and/or aggressively treated with antibiotics. A significant risk factor for IE is intravenous drug abuse. Some individuals respond well to aggressive antibiotic therapy; however, others require early or even emergent surgery (Nishimura et al., 2014). Recurrent IE is common in intravenous drug abusers (IVDAs). This paper addresses the ethical dilemma associated with repetitive valve replacements in patients who use injection drugs.

Should IVDAs be denied a second valve replacement – When is enough, enough?

DiMaio et al. (2009) published a hypothetical case of a young man in his early twenties, with two young children. The man started smoking marijuana as a teenager, and by the age of 20, he was using cocaine regularly, including intravenously. The latter led to endocarditis affecting his aortic valve, requiring open-heart surgery and valve replacement followed by a lengthy antibiotic regimen. He was warned that he would not be allowed a second valve replacement if the new valve became re-infected due to recurrent IV drug use. The patient followed up with cardiology regularly; however, eventually he started using again, his valve became re-infected and he required another valve replacement. While the patient in the aforementioned scenario was fictional, this situation is very common.

Current guidelines by the American College of Cardiology (ACC) for native and prosthetic valve endocarditis call for early surgery (Nishimura et al., 2014). The question, however, arises, whether relapsing IVDAs should be allowed a second valve. What about a third or even fourth valve replacement? Where is the line to be drawn?

DiMaio (2009) argues that noncompliance and relatively low survival rates make valve replacement surgery futile. Dr. DiMaio further states that redundant valve replacements for this patient population pose a burden on society, as resources are not unlimited. Human capital, medical supplies and labor result in high consumer costs and often times IVDAs lack health insurance and other means to pay for their surgery. A utilitarian perspective must be considered and healthcare resources should be allocated more wisely. Moreover, DiMaio (2009) argues that the entire healthcare team is at greater risk while taking care of a patient who may carry infections such as hepatitis C or HIV. Lastly, according to DiMaio (2009), surgeons have an obligation to consider circumstances, probabilities, and likely outcomes of a procedure. They do not, however, have an obligation to operate if they deem the procedure futile. DiMaio (2009) concludes that given the burden on society, the healthcare team, and a likely negative outcome like in the case of the above-described scenario, a surgeon should have the right to refuse operating.

Ethical Obligations in Todays' Healthcare System

Salerno (2009) counter-argues that the issue at hand is more complex and drug addiction should be considered a disease. Salerno argues that the patient in this case did not receive the full benefit of a comprehensive treatment plan, which would include appropriate mental health services. The patient should have been considered a dual-diagnosis patient, and rehab options should have been presented. The patient's problem is not his heart it is his drug addiction. Unless the addiction is addressed, Salerno (2009) argues, the heart cannot be repaired.

3

Salerno (2009) compares IV drug abuse to other diseases, such as diabetes, coronary artery disease, and lung cancer. Those diseases also arise from poor lifestyle choices; yet, a patient would not be denied diabetes treatment, a second or even third bypass surgery, or a lung resection. Salerno (2009) argues that the question should not be whether or not to operate, but rather whether the same surgeon is obligated to do so. Having the patient sign a contract and then deny them treatment is unethical as medical professionals are obligated to treat medical emergencies under the Hippocratic Oath. Life-threatening complications arising from IV drug abuse cannot be different from any other emergency. Poor decision-making and willing exposure to health lowering factors must not prevent patients from being treated.

Conclusion

IV drug abuse and associated medical complications including IE are a serious concern for healthcare and society. The ethical dilemma of repeated valve surgery is complex and not easy to answer. IV drug abuse should be considered a disease, such as any other disease. In order to "fix" the problem, all contributing factors must be considered. The patient's heart is not the problem whatsoever - drug addiction is. If the addiction is not addressed, any valve replacement surgery is futile, no matter if it is the patient's first surgery or subsequent operations. With that being said, many facilities offer rehabilitation options regardless of the patients' health insurance status. Some patients are eager to participate in rehabilitation while others are reluctant. Allowing patients to have endless valve replacements will ultimately result in a negative health care outcomes and cause undue burden to healthcare professional and society as a whole. Valve replacement should be mandatory once; then, if the patient fails to make an effort to pursue rehabilitation, subsequent valve replacements should be denied. I agree with the utilitarian approach and feel strongly about allocating limited resources appropriately.

References

Bor, D.H., Woolhandler, S., Nardin, R., Brusch, J., Himmelstein, D.U. (2013). Infective endocarditis in the u.s., 1998-2009: A nationwide study. *PLoS One.* doi: 10.1371/journal.pone.0060033

DiMaio, J.M., Salerno, T.A., Bernstein, R., Araujo, K., Ricci, M., & Sade, R.M. (2009). Ethical obligation of surgeons to noncompliant patients: Can a surgeon refuse to operate on an intravenous drug-abusing patient with recurrent aortic valve prosthesis infection? *The Annals of Thoracic Surgery 88*(1). doi: 10.1016/j.athoracsur.2009.03.088.

Nishimura, R. A., Otto, C. M., Bonow, R. O., Carabello, B. A., Erwin 3rd, J. P., Guyton, R. A., & ... Thomas, J. D. (2014). 2014 AHA/ACC Guideline for the management of patients with valvular heart disease: Executive summary: A report of the american college of cardiology/american heart association task force on practice guidelines. *Circulation, 129*(23), 2440-2492. doi:10.1161/CIR.0000000000000029